Live, Laugh, Love

Sydney Paige Anderson

BookLeaf
Publishing

Presentation by *BookLeaf Publishing*

Web: www.bookleafpub.com

E-mail: info@bookleafpub.com

ISBN: 9789358368048

First edition 2023

Thank you to my Mom for helping me find my voice. Thank you to my Dad who has encouraged me to explore my interests. Thank you to all of my teachers for helping me find the best in myself. A big heartfelt thank you to the teachers who truly inspired my writing: Mrs. Keezer, Mrs. Dorin, and Dr. Shepherd.

Stars Align

From sky to sea
Earth to Moon
Star to tree
You will always be
With me

The Truth May Set You Free

Dreams can end
Screams can ascend
Roses may wilt
Houses may be built
Your loved ones are with you
And my love will forever be true

Liberated

Even if all of the universe
Was filled with love
There will always be someone
Trying to shove you down

Though you may be down
I will be by your side and
I will pick you up

Your heart will be liberated
And your soul will be freed

You will stand now exhilarated
Yes, indeed

From North to South
And East to West
The seas will part
The doves will fly

Your heart is no longer tart
And neither is mine

The Golden Rule

All life is equal
No matter...
Size
Shape
Culture

But we tend to treat
Others sometimes less than we ought,
Adding unnecessary pressure
To those already struggling

Just treat others how you
Want to be treated...

Please.

Light vs. Dark

Life
Liberty
Lethargic

Cascading
Caring
Crying

Delirious
Danger
Dumbfounded

Detached
Confused
Longing

They all happen

We must accept this
We can't be afraid to feel what we feel

Live

Past
Present
Future
What did the past
Bring to the present?

What can the present
Bring to the future?

What will the future
Bring to all the people?

What will my friend

Become?
What will my family
Become?
What will I become?

The questions of life
Cannot be answered
By anyone but yourself

Live. Your. Life.
Write your own story.

Your Own

What do you do with
A blank sheet of paper?
Well, what do you do with your
Life?

Does Life find a pen and write for you?
Do YOU go find a pencil from someone else?

OR...

Do you chop down a tree?
Carve the pencil out of the wood?
Create paper from the tree?

Will your life be borrowed from someone else's
hard work,

OR...

Will you write your own story?

Who Lives Who Dies

What am I?
Who art thy?
Who are you?
What do you do?

Do you sleep all day?
Or do you go out and play?

Do you lay down and cry?
Or do you get up and try?

Thy
   Try
      To
         Die

           Or
             Thy
               Try
                 To
                   Survive

Voice

Rich
Poor

Fun
Serious

Aggressive
Passive

You
Me

Live
Hate

Life
Death

Life is full of choices...
So find your own voice
To make your own choices

Splat

A bird will fly
A cheetah will run
A laugh is fun

From here to there
We can be anywhere

Anger none
And just have fun

An amazing life can still be yours
However, don't be daft or
everything may go splat

Alienation

What are we?
Human, yes
But what are we?

Something beyond us
May call humans aliens,
While the aliens see themselves
As humans

Aliens are human?
Humans are aliens?

Is there an in-between?

Or simply equality?

Good or Evil

The World can feel evil
Love can feel evil
People can be evil

So how does Good actually win?

Because even though
EVIL
Tries its best to create havoc....

There is still good in
Everyone
And
Everything

There is good in
Our world
And love
And people

We could push all evil away,
If we try
If we really try
To just be good

Schooled

School is hard, and
You just want to play
in the yard

Some don't get it
Some do

Balance
Is your talent

You are smart
So you and I will never part

You are kind and
So am I, so
You and I will fill our time
Doing amazing things with our lives

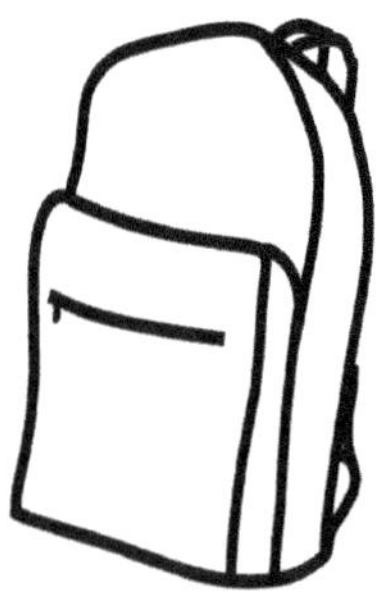

Orchard

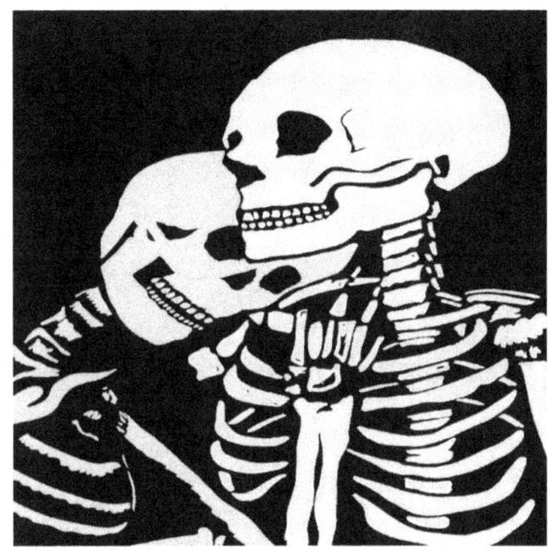

In the sky
We heard a cry
Beauty was in the air

However,
Something was askew
In the orchard

An apple tortured
In the orchard
But by whom?
Was it a crew?

Was it the crow?
Was it the apple pickers?
Was it that child who picked the apple
and threw it down on the ground as not worthy?

Are they alive?
Are we alive?

Will they survive?
Will we just survive, or
become our most delicious selves?

Suns from the Heavens

Look for our Sun
Don't worry,
I won't make a pun
Just please hurry...

Otherwise, you may miss sunrise and
Basking in its warmth and beauty

Do you deny its power to command smiles
and happy thoughts?

Pictures are worth a thousand
Words they say, and special
Memories in your brain are bound to stay

Pray thanks to the Heavens for making all of the
Suns

Unstoppable

Respect is earned
Not given until...
after many things learned and
Lots of livin'

Debates are all fun
And games
Until you see the
Pains and gains

The liars
The cheats
The jerks

You must sort through
Them all to have a ball

Push forward...
Break through...
Pursue your dreams...

Become unstoppable

Polar Opposites

Day and night
Wrong or right
Same and opposite
Genuine and hypocrite

Poem or paragraph
Twin or single
Deed or devil
Favor or debt

Life is full of possibilities
Including lies
Don't be unwise

Believe

Take care of the weak
The lost
The unwanted
The unqualified
The unhinged
The un-homed

And make them strong
Make them more
Found
Wanted
Loved
Homed

Make them believe in
Themselves
Others
Goodness
Kindness
Faith
Love
God

Make them their own

Spark

Be the light in the dark
The spark in the flame
The good in the house
The mercy in the room
The hope for the homeless

You will be the good who
Denounces evil and
Be the kindness that rises
From the ashes

Too late
Not enough
Weak
Homeless

No

Strong
Persevere
Brave
Wise

You are you
Don't change who you are ... EVER

Defeat - Rejected

Defeat?
No. Never.

They may never seem to want you
They may never seem to see you
They may never seem to be there for you

Don't Listen
Don't accept

Don't be....
A cheater
A liar
A virus
Here to wipe out

Anyone's capability to
Love and be loved

Defeat - Rejected!

All in the Name of Love

It's all in the name of
Love...
Everything we do
Everything we say

But why?
Why give in?
Why surrender?

I'll tell you why...
For good feelings
For reassurance
For well-being

Because we all need love

Hear me
Hear my cry for you
I want to hear your voice
Calling for me

For it's all in the name of
Love